A Robbie Reader

MONEY MATTERS: A KID'S GUIDE TO MONEY

A KID'S GUIDE TO THE ECONOMY

Tamra Orr

Mitchell Lane

PUBLISHERS

P.O. Box 196
Hockessin, Delaware 19707
Visit us on the web: www.mitchelllane.com
Comments? email us: mitchelllane@mitchelllane.com

Mitchell Lane
PUBLISHERS

MONEY MATTERS
A KID'S GUIDE TO MONEY

Budgeting Tips for Kids

Coins and Other Currency

A Kid's Guide to Earning Money

A Kid's Guide to Stock Market Investing

A Kid's Guide to the Economy

Savings Tips for Kids

Copyright © 2010 by Mitchell Lane Publishers

ABOUT THE AUTHOR: Tamra Orr is the author of almost 200 books for children of all ages. She lives in the Pacific Northwest with her four kids and husband. Like everyone else, 2009 has taught her to pay a great deal more attention to how the economy works. She has learned how decisions in the White House can affect her own daily life—and reads the financial section of her local newspaper much closer than she used to.

**Library of Congress
Cataloging-in-Publication Data**

Orr, Tamra.
  A kid's guide to the economy / by Tamra Orr.
      p. cm. — (Money matters: a kid's guide to money)
  Includes bibliographical references and index.
  ISBN 978-1-58415-836-3 (library bound)
  1. Economics—Juvenile literature. I. Title.
  HB183.O77 2010
  330—dc22
                                        2009027326

PUBLISHER'S NOTE: The facts on which the story in this book is based have been thoroughly researched. Documentation of such research can be found on page 46. While every possible effort has been made to ensure accuracy, the publisher will not assume liability for damages caused by inaccuracies in the data, and makes no warranty on the accuracy of the information contained herein.

Printing   2   3   4   5   6   7   8   9

Contents

Words in **bold** type can be found in the glossary.

BUSINE

THE WALL STREET

OUT OF THE HEADLINES

The hallways of Madison Elementary School were loud and busy. Students yelled back and forth. Locker doors slammed shut. Hundreds of feet pounded the floor. The sounds bounced off the walls, echoing and making them louder.

The first morning bell rang just as Connor strolled into Mrs. Clarkson's classroom. "Hey, Tashia," he said, sliding into his seat. "Are you still planning to go to the movies this weekend?"

"No," replied Tashia with a sigh. "I want to, but my mom keeps saying we have to cut back 'in this economy.' I have no idea what she is talking about! What is the deal with the economy?"

"When my father says stuff like that, I think it means we have to watch our spending more closely," suggested Connor. "But what our money has to do with the economy, I have no idea."

"And what does any of it have to do with going to the movies?" asked Tashia.

Money Makers

Sometimes Mother Nature can change the economy. Natural disasters such as earthquakes, floods, tornadoes, and hurricanes can make it hard for businesses to stay open, people to get to work, and products to be made and sold. Human-caused disasters such as wars can have different effects on the economy. World War II created so many jobs, it helped pull the nation out of the Great Depression. On the other hand, the modern War in Iraq has created huge levels of debt for the country.

"Okay, everyone. Let's get started," Mrs. Clarkson announced to the noisy classroom. She quickly took attendance. Then she sat on her desk and smiled at her students.

"We are going to start on a new project today. I have heard many of you talking about the economy lately." Connor blushed and Tashia slid down in her seat. "And I think you have a lot of questions about it," the teacher continued.

"It seems like the economy is all they talk about on the news anymore," said Carrie.

"I hear about it at school, at home, and on television," added Sean. "The other night, my parents talked about it throughout dinner. I tried to follow along, but I got lost pretty quickly."

"The economy is always a big topic," agreed Mrs. Clarkson. "And that is one of the main things we will

During the Great Depression, families had to struggle just to put food on the table and clothes on their backs. It took a toll on everyone, including children.

discuss in class. We will look at how the economy works and how it affects people's lives."

Walking to the blackboard at the front of the room, the teacher picked up a piece of chalk. "When you hear people talking about the economy," she said, "what words do you usually hear? Let's make a list of them."

"I heard my mom say something to my grandfather about a **recession** the other day," said Pedro. Mrs. Clarkson nodded and wrote the word on the board.

"My uncle Leo was talking about the **Great Depression** just last week," added Carrie. "I think that happened a long time ago, so I am not sure if it has anything to do with what is going on today or not."

"That reminds me of a famous saying," said Mrs. Clarkson. "I believe it says, 'Those who do not understand the past are often doomed to repeat it.' It means that learning about events that happened in the past—such as the Great Depression—can help you better understand the present." She added *depression* to the list.

Sean raised his hand. "I was watching TV last night. They were talking about something they called **inflation**. I could tell it had something to do with the economy, but I don't know what exactly."

Mrs. Clarkson nodded again and wrote the word on the board. "That's a good one," she said.

As the class chatted about different economic terms, the list grew and grew. The longer the students thought about it, the more words they realized they had heard somewhere before. By the time class was almost over, Mrs. Clarkson had written ten different terms on the blackboard:

Recession	Depression
Inflation	Unemployment
Supply	Demand
Goods	Services
Market	Bailout

"Good job, everyone. This is a great start," said Mrs. Clarkson. "It gives us some terms to discuss and learn about. For now, it's best to understand that the word *economy* simply means the way a government and businesses work together in order to provide people with the goods and services they want. I will talk more about that in the next few weeks. In the meantime, I have an assignment to get you started over the weekend. I want you to write down each of the words on the board. Then, for the next few days, anytime you hear one of them mentioned anywhere, by anyone, make a mark by the word. Let's see how often they really are being discussed!"

Tashia raised her hand. "Mrs. Clarkson, I have a request. Can you make going to the movies over the weekend part of the assignment?"

Everyone laughed, including the teacher. "I wish I could," Mrs. Clarkson replied, "but I'm afraid your parents might not appreciate that. After all . . ." She paused and looked at her class expectantly.

"We know, we know," said Tashia. "We have to be careful 'in this economy.' I have to admit, I am anxious to finally find out what that means!"

Mrs. Clarkson smiled. "I will do my best," she said. Just then, the class bell rang.

As Connor headed out of the classroom, he waited by the door for Tashia. "Good try," he said, with a grin.

Tashia grinned back. "What can I say? Going to the movies is one homework assignment I would actually want to do!"

THE BASICS OF ECONOMICS

If you pay close attention, you will find that the words *economy* and *economics* are used all the time. You will hear the terms on the nightly news. You will hear them in school. They will pop up in the local newspaper and national magazines. Chances are, you may even hear at least a few of them in your house as finances are discussed over the phone or across the dinner table.

The word *economy* comes from ancient Greece. It means "management of a household or a business." Today, the term means much more than that. It usually means the management of entire countries. Economies can be local (in your city or state), national (in your country as a whole), and global (worldwide).

Before you can define *economy*, you will need to understand some terms. The first one is **goods**. Goods are things that are made, sold, and bought by people like you. They include the compact disc you bought at the bookstore, the pair of jeans from the department store, the sandwich from the fast-food restaurant, and the tube of toothpaste from the pharmacy. Goods are items you can buy and use.

Another term to know is **services**. These are things that one person pays another person or group of people to do. For example, a person pays the mechanic who fixes his car, the police officer who patrols the streets, the firefighter who douses a blazing house, and the many doctors and nurses who take care of a patient's illness or

GOODS

SERVICES

COMMODITIES

injury. If you have ever been paid to baby-sit, shovel snow from a driveway, deliver a newspaper, or walk a dog, you have been paid for providing a service.

Think about the people you know who have jobs. Where do they work? What do they do? Do those jobs involve goods or services?

Understanding what goods and services are is the first step to understanding how an economy works. The actual definition of *economics* is the study of how all of these **commodities** are bought, sold, and used. Economics uses information about what products are made and what services are provided, as well as who buys these things and how many they purchase.

Economies can be strong or weak, sick or healthy. They can go up. They can go down. They do this over and over in a cycle that we will explore more in another chapter. How well an economy is doing in any country is measured by a special number called the **Gross Domestic Product**, or GDP. The number shows the value of a country's goods and services produced within a one-year period. It includes whatever taxes pay for as well, such as public schooling, road maintenance, and the armed services. These numbers are often so huge that they are measured in trillions of dollars. In 2008, the U.S. had the second biggest GDP in the world, with $14.3 trillion. (The largest is the European Union, at $14.8 trillion!) According to *The World Factbook*, the second biggest was China at $7.8 trillion, and the smallest was Tokelau, a territory in New Zealand. Its 2008 GDP was only $1.5 million.

A term that sounds a lot like the GDP is the GNP, or **Gross National Product**. It measures the total value of goods and services too, but includes whatever the country may produce in other countries as well.

Money Makers

The World Factbook reports: The ten countries that have the largest GNPs are, in order of size, the United States, Japan, Germany, China, Great Britain, France, Italy, Spain, Canada, and India.

Recreation

Health Care

Education

Housing

Food

Transportation

Other

Goods and Services That Contribute to the Gross Domestic Product

A Look Back in Time

To understand how any economy works now, it helps to look at the past. The idea of an economy like the one in the United States today did not really exist until a few centuries ago. Native Americans had an entirely different type of economy because they **bartered** and shared their goods and services. All of that changed when settlers came from Europe. They brought many new ideas with them, including a new way of making and selling products.

The colonists who left Europe to settle in North America started their own economy also. While they continued to barter with the Native Americans, they also made money by selling furs to people in Europe. Soon, sawmills were built. Shipyards produced trading vessels and fishing boats. Plantations grew crops that were sold to others.

In the early 1800s, steam-powered machines were invented and improved. They made a huge difference in America's

Buffalo pelt

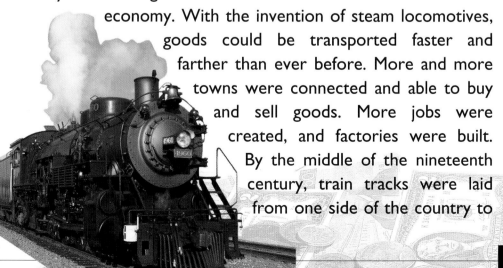

economy. With the invention of steam locomotives, goods could be transported faster and farther than ever before. More and more towns were connected and able to buy and sell goods. More jobs were created, and factories were built. By the middle of the nineteenth century, train tracks were laid from one side of the country to the other, and countless towns were born in between. In 1885, the gas-powered automobile was invented, creating a worldwide demand for oil. By 1914, cars were being mass-produced in several of the country's largest cities.

Since then, the U.S. economy has gone through many changes. It has gone up—and down. It has soared into times of amazing **prosperity** and then plummeted to times of terrible depression. During the late 1920s and into the early

The assembly line changed the economy and how goods were manufactured. In 1913, Henry Ford's company mass-produced the country's first automobiles, a procedure that continues today—although with more machines and fewer people.

United States Unemployment Rates 1950–2008
(Source: United States Department of Labor)

Over the last half century, unemployment rates have gone up and down as much as the typical roller coaster! In 2009, the rate was rapidly reaching an all-time high—but history has shown that it would improve again.

1940s, for example, the country's economy was under tremendous stress. Those years came to be known as the Great Depression. Many families lost entire fortunes. More people were out of work than ever before. People stood in line for bread and other food, and many people starved. It was a sad and difficult time. It took many years for the economy to recover.

There has not been another terrible economic depression in the United States since the one that hit in the fall of 1929. The country has come close a few times, and in 2009, it came closer than ever before. Knowing what made things better and worse 70 years earlier has helped modern **economists**—the experts who study how economies work—know what to do and what not to do.

MEET SUPPLY AND DEMAND

More than 100 years ago, an Englishman named Alfred Marshall wrote a book about economics. In it, he explained one of the most basic ideas involved in the economy: **the law of supply and demand**. That same idea is still used today.

Imagine that you are exceptionally good at math. You get A's on all of your assignments and tests. Working with numbers just comes easily to you, and you even look forward to doing your math homework. Now, imagine that you are also good at teaching others how to understand math. Your ability to teach another person how to do math well is a service you could supply through tutoring. Pretend that your usual price for tutoring someone is $10 an hour. However, what if there was going to be a school-wide math test next month?

Any student who didn't get a good score on it would have to repeat a grade. You might find yourself with a dozen or more students clamoring for your time and teaching skills. This shows that the **demand** for your services has gone up. On the other hand, what if you are the *only* math tutor in the whole school? This means there is a **scarcity** of tutors—and it means you are not only in demand but will leave many students frustrated because there is not enough of you to go around!

If that happens, what can you do? You can raise your fee of $10 an hour. Students are desperate for the help you can give them, and as their demand goes up, so does your **supply**—and your price. You might charge $15 or $20 an hour now. If you were a business, you would report that you were making a great **profit** or income.

But . . . what would happen if that school-wide math test was canceled? Suddenly, the demand would drop. (Students wouldn't need you nearly as much! They might be worried about their grades, but they would no longer be cramming for that test.) Price and supply would also have to drop. You would be back to $10 an hour—and if the demand dropped enough, you would have to cut your hours.

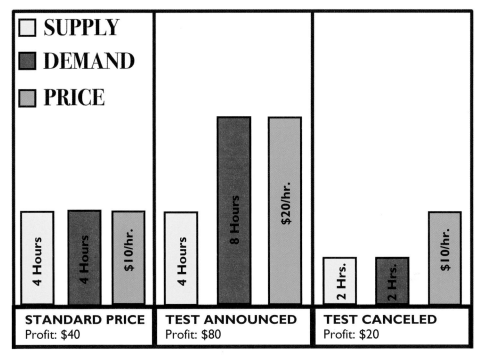

SUPPLY	DEMAND	PRICE

STANDARD PRICE
Profit: $40
4 Hours | 4 Hours | $10/hr.

TEST ANNOUNCED
Profit: $80
4 Hours | 8 Hours | $20/hr.

TEST CANCELED
Profit: $20
2 Hrs. | 2 Hrs. | $10/hr.

Remember that supply can be a service (such as tutoring) or an actual product. For example, what if you made the most amazing friendship bracelets? You could supply (make and sell) them to other students, friends, and family. As word spread, demand for your product might go up, and more and more people would want to buy them. If you had been charging $5 each, you could raise the price to $7.50 or even $10. If you used only $3 worth of materials for each one, you would be making a good profit on each sale. Since you were the only one making the bracelets, you would have a **monopoly** on the business. What would happen though, if someone else at school began making fantastic friendship bracelets too? Chances are, because of the **competition**, your demand would drop, your sales would go down, and you would have to lower your prices to try to lure customers back. If you charged less

The Effect of Bracelet Competition

No Competitors	One Competitor	Two Competitors

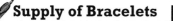 **Supply of Bracelets**   **Demand for Bracelets**   **Sale Price**

When the supply of friendship bracelets is less than the demand, you can pick the price you want to charge. When supply equals demand, prices will drop. When supply is greater than demand, prices may be forced to go below the cost of making the product. When this happens, it will be too expensive to make them anymore.

than $3 each, however, what would that mean? Instead of making a profit, you would be losing money instead. How many bracelets could you keep making if it was costing you money instead of earning it? The answer is—not many. You would run out of materials, and then what would you use to buy more?

In the Business World

The law of supply and demand in today's economy works basically the same way as in the school examples above. When the demand for something goes up, the supply and the price go up. When the demand falls, so do supply and price. Just as in the example with friendship bracelets, when one company completely controls the market, that company has a monopoly. If that company has competition from another business, however, it affects supply and demand and can result in cutting a profit—or putting a company out of business.

Have you ever seen the law of supply and demand at work in the economy? What happens when a new video game for an electronic game system comes out? People stand in line to buy a copy—even camping out all night to be sure they get one. How much does the game sell for? Usually it has a very high price, because the manufacturer, or the company that made it, knows that demand is very high at first. They can charge high prices— and make a huge profit. But what happens a few months later when many people have bought a copy and have been playing the game for weeks? You will see used copies popping up for sale at much lower prices. Demand for the game goes down—and so do the price and supply.

The United States has a **free market economy**. This means that both the people who are selling a product or a service and the people who are choosing to buy that product or service are doing so through free choice. No one is telling them what to make or what to charge. No one is forcing them to buy or not to buy something. No one is stopping another company from offering the very same products at a different price, either (monopolies are illegal in the United

Being in a free market forces stores to compete with each other for business. This, in turn, becomes a huge advantage for the consumer, as stores have to keep prices down and have sales in order to attract customers.

States). The only law that drives businesses in a free market economy is the law of supply and demand.

This type of market is not found in some other countries, however. A **command economy**, for instance, is one in which the government controls what is produced, how it is to be used, what price tag should be on products and services, and where the money earned from selling them goes. In the past, both Russia and China operated under this type of economy. In 2009, command economies were still in operation in North Korea and Cuba.

Some economies are considered **mixed**, which means a combination of free market and command. It blends private businesses with government-controlled ones. Some remote cultures such as those of the Aborigines in Australia and some Amazon tribes also operate on a barter economy. Goods and services are exchanged for one another instead of for money. It is a type of swapping.

Knowing how supply and demand work is a key to understanding how the economy works. Nothing will exchange hands without those two important factors!

In Cuba, dictator Fidel Castro (left) told the people what to produce, how much of it they needed, how much they could charge for it, and where the money was to go. When his brother, Raul Castro, became president in 2008, he began to reform Cuba's economy.

25

Chapter 4

A NEVER-ENDING CYCLE

Have you ever noticed that some things follow each other without fail? January and February are always followed by March. Ten P.M. is always followed by eleven P.M. and then midnight.

The seasons are like this, too. Each year, spring is followed by summer, autumn, and then, finally, winter. They follow a cycle of nature that never changes or comes to an end. The economy also tends to follow a set cycle that does not really end. And, just as no one can predict the exact moment when the snowflakes will stop and spring breezes will start to blow, no one can predict exactly when one economic phase will stop and the next one will begin. A lot of people keep trying to, though!

Also like the changing seasons of the year, there is no beginning or end to the economic cycle. There is no true starting place. Although we will look at each of the phases—**expansion**, prosperity, recession, and **recovery**—it is essential to understand that none of them "comes first." They just go around and around in a circle. They are always in the same order, but precisely how long each one lasts varies every single time.

Let's look at each of the phases in the economic cycle. As you read about them, think about what you have learned about the economy so far and see which phase seems to fit what is happening right now.

A Time of Expansion

We'll begin by explaining the phase of the economic cycle known as expansion. Some economists refer to it as a period of boom. This is definitely a growing time for the economy. New businesses open, which creates new jobs for workers. People feel good and confident about their work and about what they are buying. Many couples buy their first house. Some **entrepreneurs** start their own companies. Some invest in stocks for the first time. Companies sell to other companies across the country, and to other countries around the world. The GDP grows quickly. This phase is the most hopeful one. It is one in which people tend to look ahead and see a bright and sunny future.

Welcome to Prosperity

The next phase is prosperity. During this phase, everything that was hoped for during the expansion phase is happening. Businesses thrive. Unemployment is down. Incomes are up. **Interest rates**, the percentage people have to pay on money they borrow from banks and other credit institutions, go up. People begin to spend money almost as fast as they earn it. This means that the government has to print more of it—and that causes an economic problem called **inflation**. Since demand for goods is high, prices go up. When prices go up, people use more money, more bills are printed, and inflation occurs. People begin to get a little nervous. Storm clouds are on the horizon. They signal the beginning of the next phase.

Money Makers

The use of personal computers in millions of homes all over the world has had a big effect on the economy. Anyone who has an Internet connection can buy and sell virtually anything with nothing more than a few clicks of the mouse! On the other hand, because it is easier to make purchases from one's home, retailers—actual stores—have suffered.

Expansion

Prosperity

Down into Recession

The third phase is typically referred to as recession. It happens when the economy slows down and stays that way for more than six months. People start watching their spending more closely. They begin to worry. They cut back on luxuries such as eating out in restaurants, spending time shopping, and going to the movies. They also stop purchasing big-ticket items such as cars and houses. Instead, they spend money on day-to-day needs such as gas for their cars, food for their families, and housing and utility payments. Because consumers are spending less, businesses start cutting back, and employee hours are reduced. Unemployment starts to

Recovery

Recession

rise. The GDP drops. Inflation begins to slow because people are holding on to their money instead of spending it. The downpour is about to start.

Often the recession phase is accompanied by the collapse or failure of some type of major business. In 2001, the United States suffered through a recession when many dot-com businesses, or Internet-based companies, collapsed. The recession deepened after the terrorist attacks on New York's Twin Towers and D.C.'s Pentagon on September 11, 2001. It took many months of struggling to move toward the last phase in the cycle.

In late 2008, another recession began. This time it was spearheaded by a combination of the collapse of the real estate or housing market, and the closing of multiple banks across the country. Newly elected President Barack Obama worked to help the country recover through a massive **bailout** plan.

Time for Recovery

The fourth phase of the economic cycle is recovery. In response to the problems of inflation and recession, the government usually steps in to help improve the economy. They lower both taxes and interest rates. This eases the pressure on people and businesses by freeing up some of their money. Slowly, confidence returns. People feel better about the future and begin spending money again. Jobs open up once more, so unemployment rates drop. People feel more 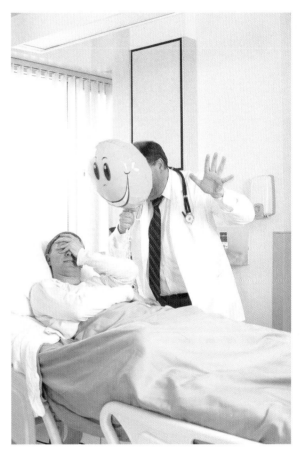 secure about borrowing money from banks and about using their credit cards. Over the months, this phase circles back to expansion, and the entire cycle begins again. The sunshine begins peeking through the clouds, and blue skies are on their way back.

The Federal Reserve in Washington, D.C., is headquarters for all of the banks in the United States. It was first created in 1913 under President Woodrow Wilson. It was not an easy process—many people were against the idea of a centralized bank. Finally, in November 1914, the Federal Reserve opened for business, just before World War I erupted across the globe.

Learning about the four phases of this constant cycle can help you understand what the economy is doing at any given time. Think about what is happening in businesses today. Now that you know about this cycle, where do you think the U.S. economy is right now? What clues have you seen to help you figure out the answer? Make a list and ask yourself: Are we in expansion, prosperity, recession, or recovery?

Chapter 5

COPING WITH A CHANGING ECONOMY

The economy is a common topic because it affects everyone. Whether the economy is up or down, entering the expansion phase or leaving the recession phase, the economy is a popular subject of conversation. Politicians talk about it constantly. Newspaper reporters write about it daily. Radio program hosts interview people about it frequently. Experts study it endlessly.

In good times, people talk about the wisest investments to make and the best new businesses to open. They make confident plans for the future. In the lean times, on the other hand, they talk about how to cope with the uncertainty and the best ways to save money. They focus on making it until the next payday. There is no question that regardless of what the economy is doing at any moment, people will be talking about it.

Obviously, when the economy is strong, life is usually much easier. Many families are less concerned about whether they can pay bills or go on vacation. Businesses are more

During leaner times, many families search for ways to save money. One popular choice during the summer is to not travel and instead have a staycation. In this instance, parents and kids have fun without leaving home. It often includes exploring a nearby city for fun activities, having friends over for parties or get-togethers, and opting for picnics and barbecues instead of eating out.

interested in purchasing new equipment, hiring new workers, or opening additional stores. It is a different picture when the economy is struggling, however. Daily life at home often becomes difficult. A shaky economy creates challenges that many families have no choice but to learn how to deal with. Often these challenges are like a row of dominoes. Once the first one goes over, the rest of them go tumbling down.

Following the Dominoes

As you learned in the previous chapter, when recession starts, unemployment grows. Throughout the country, thousands— and sometimes millions—of jobs can be lost in a matter of months. It is not unusual for a mother's or father's job to suddenly be in danger. In an attempt to save money on **payroll**, employers frequently cut their employees' hours or lay off multiple workers, even if it is only temporary. In Delaware in 2009, for example, there was a proposal to cut teachers'

In difficult economic times, as business profits drop, stock prices fall. People's investments can lose value. For older people who have invested money as part of their retirement plans, as stocks drop in value, the money they have to live on falls, too.

salaries by 8 percent—without reducing their workload. Many companies cut back on how many hours they will be open so they will not have to pay employees to work those times. Even community centers and public libraries find they have to limit their hours. Cutting employees' paychecks reduces the money coming into a household every month—and that can start those economic dominoes falling.

While in better times, banks might have been willing to let people suffering a financial setback borrow money, during a recession, this is far less true. The banks become careful too, so they make fewer loans. Instead, families may have to rely on any money they might have in savings accounts or other investments, such as retirement plans.

Families may have to change where they live also. **Mortgage** payments, or the money paid monthly on a bank loan given

When people's retirement plans begin to lose value, the retired may have no choice but to go back into the workforce—a prospect that is rarely welcomed and, in times of high unemployment, is also very difficult to do.

As the housing market fell, there were more houses on the market than there were buyers. The demand for housing dropped, prices went down, and home values plummeted.

in order to buy a house, can suddenly become impossible to make. It is easy to fall behind and then not be able to catch up. When a person falls too far behind on the mortgage, the bank can take the house. This is called **foreclosure**. When this happens, the people in the house must find somewhere else to live. To stay on top of their bills, people may choose to move from large houses to smaller homes or apartments, which tend to cost quite a bit less per month. However, in tough economic times, there are fewer buyers for those large houses, and the original owner has to keep coming up with those crippling payments.

The struggle to keep up with mortgage payments played a large role in the 2008–2009 recession. Many banks failed, in part because the people they had loaned money to simply

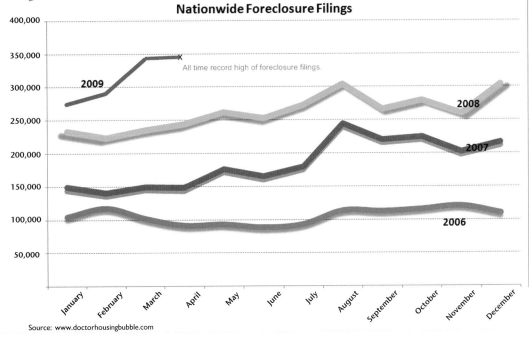

Nationwide Foreclosure Filings

All time record high of foreclosure filings.

2009

2008

2007

2006

Source: www.doctorhousingbubble.com

From late 2007 through 2009, more and more people fell behind on their mortgage payments. As banks foreclosed on these houses, they made less and less profit. Lenders were forced to either go out of business or accept government bailout funds.

were not earning enough to pay them back. There were so many houses on the market, their value dropped, and banks were not able to make back the money they had loaned.

In 2008, an act was passed by Congress that allowed the U.S. Department of the Treasury to give up to $700 billion to American banks that were struggling. They did so in the hopes of getting the banks back on their feet and helping the economy. The plan was often referred to as a bailout. Meanwhile, the Federal Reserve Board reduced interest rates, making home ownership more affordable. The government focused a great deal of attention and time on helping people so that in another domino effect, the housing market—and thus the economy—could bounce back once again.

While a slow economy can make life hard, the economy is always changing. One phase is sure to shift to the next one. In other words—things will get better. In the meantime, what can you do? Here are a some ideas for making tough times easier for you and your family:

- If you are confused or upset about what is happening with the economy, talk to somebody about it. Ask your parents questions. Talk to your teachers. Share your feelings and thoughts.

- Be patient with your parents and other adults who may be under extra stress.

- Help out around the house to support your parents. Ask your family often what you can do to help.

- Keep up with your schoolwork. That will be one less thing to worry about.

- Find ways to spend time having fun without spending money, such as playing games, reading books, riding bikes, or talking to friends.

- Eat healthy food and get enough sleep—those two make absolutely everything easier to handle.

- Volunteer to help others with baby-sitting, running errands, doing yard work, and more.

- Donate your unwanted items such as books, toys, or clothes to thrift stores, which can pass them on to those in need.

- Get the facts—not the rumors. Read your local newspaper and watch the news to get updates on the economy. But don't listen to the rumors and opinions of others, because they are rarely true and are often exaggerated.

GOING GREEN

On Monday morning, everyone in Mrs. Clarkson's class was excited to share how many times they had heard some of the different economic terms over the weekend.

Mrs. Clarkson put the list on the blackboard one more time. As each student read off the numbers they had written next to the terms, the teacher kept a running tally. The most common word was *economy*, followed by *recession* and *bailout*. Many students had heard their families using these terms, while others had heard them on television and radio or spotted them in newspaper headlines.

"I heard the word *economy* almost a dozen times," said Carrie, looking over her list. She grinned. "My dad is the accountant for a company, so I tend to hear it all the time."

"I heard *unemployment* the most," admitted Connor. "My uncle Bill was over and he has been job searching for a couple of weeks. He says it is very hard to find work right now."

Tashia raised her hand. "I heard a term that was not on the list," she stated. "I heard the word *green* the most."

CHAPTER 6

Everyone looked confused for a moment. Tashia explained. "The reason I heard that is because my mom got a new job! She was hired last Friday. She is going to be the receptionist for a local business that makes solar panels for houses and small companies. She was learning about the products, and she and my dad were talking about the environment. I guess that one of the ways to improve the economy—and the world—is to go green with energy-saving products like windmills, electric cars, and solar panels."

As some businesses fold, others are created. More and more employers are looking for ways to support the environment, and this often results in a wider choice of jobs for people.

Installing windmills is one method some farmers and other business owners have chosen to generate electricity, save money, and help the planet. The technology behind these changes has helped create new jobs as well.

"That's terrific, Tashia," said Mrs. Clarkson. "New jobs are good news in this economy."

"Yes—and hey, I even got to see a movie," Tashia added, with a grin. "Of course, it was a DVD at home about how solar energy and wind power work—but at least we still made popcorn to go with it!"

For Young Readers
Books

Allman, Barbara. *Banking: How Economics Works.* Minneapolis, Minnesota: Lerner Publications, 2005.

Challen, Paul. *How Do Mortgages, Loans and Credit Work?* New York: Crabtree Publishing Company, 2009.

Craats, Rennay. *Economy.* New York: Weigl Publishers, 2008.

Gilman, Laura Anne. *Economics: How Economics Works.* Minneapolis, Minnesota: Lerner Publications, 2006.

Hiber, Amanda. *Do Tax Breaks Benefit the Economy?* Farmington Hills, Michigan: Greenhaven Press, 2009.

Hunnicut, Susan. *What Is the Future of the U.S. Economy?* Farmington Hills, Michigan: Greenhaven Press, 2008.

Kiyosaki, Robert. *Rich Dad, Poor Dad for Teens: The Secrets about Money That You Don't Learn in School.* Philadelphia: Running Press, 2009.

Web Sites for Kids

Economy for Kids
http://www2.scholastic.com/ browse/collection.jsp?id=455

Social Studies for Kids: Economics
http://www.socialstudiesforkids. com/subjects/economics.htm

You Are Here (consumerism for kids)
http://www.ftc.gov/youarehere/

Young Money: Student Entrepreneurs
http://www.youngmoney. com/entrepreneur/student_ entrepreneurs

Works Consulted
Books

Ayers, Ronald and Robert Collinge. *Economics: Explore and Apply.* Saddle River, New Jersey: Pearson Education, 2004.

Cleaver, Tony. *Understanding the World Economy.* Florence, Kentucky: Routledge Books, 2006.

Glencoe, McGraw-Hill Economics: Today and Tomorrow. Blacklick, Ohio: Glencoe/McGraw-Hill, 2007.

Harford, Tim. *The Undercover Economist.* New York: Random House, 2007.

Slavin, Steve. *Economics: A Self-Teaching Guide.* New York: John Wiley and Sons, 2000.

Sowell, Thomas. *Basic Economics: A Common Sense Guide to the Economy,* Third Edition. Jackson, Tennessee: Basic Books, 2007.

Teller-Elsberg, Jonathan. *Field Guide to the U.S. Economy: A Compact and Irreverent Guide to Economic Life in America.* New York: New Press, 2006.

On the Internet

Baker, Samuel L., Ph.D. University of South Carolina: Economics Interactive Tutorials
http://hadm.sph.sc.edu/Courses/ Econ/Tutorials.html

Fed 101
http://www. federalreserveeducation.org

Forbes. Investopedia's Economics Basics: Introduction
http://www.investopedia.com/ university/economics/

Moody's Economy
http://www.economy.com/default.asp

The White House's Economy Report
http://www.whitehouse.gov/issues/ economy/

bailout—A government loan given to businesses to help them avoid going bankrupt.

barter—To trade one good or service for another.

command economy—An economy in which the government controls what is produced and sold.

commodities (kuh-MAH-dih-tees)—Goods and services.

competition (kom-peh-TIH-shun)—Two or more businesses or individuals who produce the same goods or services and compete for customers.

demand—How much need or want there is for a good or service.

economist (ee-KAH-nuh-mist)—A person who has been especially educated in how economies work.

entrepreneurs (on-truh-preh-NOORS)—Individuals who have innovative ideas for businesses or products.

expansion (ek-SPAN-shun)—The phase in an economic cycle that is characterized by growth.

foreclosure (for-KLOH-jhur)—To end the terms of a mortgage agreement, with the property returning to the lender.

free market economy—An economy in which people are free to buy and sell as they choose.

goods—Things that are bought and sold.

Great Depression—A period in history (1929–1939) during which many people lost their jobs and savings, resulting in poverty, hunger, and other problems.

Gross Domestic Product (GDP)—The value of a country's goods and services produced within that country within a year.

Gross National Product (GNP)—The value of a country's goods and services produced around the world within a year.

inflation (in-FLAY-shun)—The drop in the value of currency that occurs when the government prints too much money.

interest rate—The amount the loan company or bank charges someone for borrowing money.

law of supply and demand—The economic law that states when demand goes up, so does supply.

mixed economy—An economy that merges free market and command economy philosophies.

monopoly (muh-NAH-puh-lee)—A market in which a seller has no competition.

mortgage (MOR-gidj)—A bank loan against the value of something, such as a house.

payroll—The wages a company pays its employees.

profit (PRAH-fit)—Money earned that is above what supplies and labor cost to make or produce a good or service.

prosperity (prah-SPAYR-ih-tee)—The phase in an economic cycle that is characterized by profit and growth.

recession (ree-SEH-shun)—When the economy slows down for a period of six months or more.

recovery (ree-KUH-vuh-ree)—The phase in an economic cycle in which the government lowers taxes and interest rates to bolster the economy.

scarcity (SKAYR-sih-tee)—A shortage or lack of a supply.

services—Things one person pays another to do for him or her.

supply—The amount of a good or service that is available.

Index